TERRORISM IN TODAY'S WORLD

Pan Am 103
and State-Sponsored Terrorism

MICHAEL G. PAUL

CURRICULUM CONSULTANT: MICHAEL M. YELL
National Board Certified Social Studies Teacher,
Hudson Middle School, Hudson, Wisconsin

WORLD ALMANAC® LIBRARY

Please visit our web site at: www.worldalmanaclibrary.com
For a free color catalog describing World Almanac® Library's list of high-quality books
and multimedia programs, call 1-800-848-2928 (USA) or 1-800-387-3178 (Canada).
World Almanac® Library's fax: (414) 332-3567.

Library of Congress Cataloging-in-Publication Data

Paul, Michael.
    Pan Am 103 and state-sponsored terrorism / Michael Paul.
      p. cm. — (Terrorism in today's world)
    Includes bibliographical references and index.
    ISBN 0-8368-6559-6 (lib. bdg.)
    ISBN 0-8368-6566-9 (softcover)
    1. Pan Am Flight 103 Bombing Incident, 1988—Juvenile literature.
2. Terrorism—United States—Juvenile literature. 3. Terrorism—Europe—Juvenile
literature. 4. Bombing investigation—Scotland—Lockerbie—Juvenile literature.
5. Terrorism—Government policy—Juvenile literature. I. Title. II. Series.
    HV6431.P387   2006
    327.1'17—dc22
                                 2005056969

This North American edition first published in 2006 by
World Almanac® Library
A Member of the WRC Media Family of Companies
330 West Olive Street, Suite 100
Milwaukee, WI 53212 USA

Original edition copyright © 2004 The Brown Reference Group plc. This U.S. edition
copyright © 2006 by World Almanac® Library.

Managing Editor: Tim Cooke
Designer: Steve Wilson
Picture Researcher: Laila Torsun
World Almanac® Library editor: Alan Wachtel
World Almanac® Library art direction: Tammy West
World Almanac® Library design: Dave Kowalski
World Almanac® Library production: Jessica Morris and Robert Kraus

Picture credits: Front cover: Topham BRG: 06; Corbis: Kashi, Ed 40; Reuters 39; Staveris,
S/Aperion 26/27; Stewart, Mike 21; Empics: Abaca Press 28, Bacon, Chris 22; Frances;
Sian/AP 23; PA 14; Rousseau, Stefan/PA 43; Getty: Karp, Cindy 34; Mary Evans: 31; Rex:
Kidd, Tom 10; Sipa Press 11, 19, 32; Zabci, Mr. F. 16; Topham: 04/05, 15; US Navy
Photo: 36/37

Printed in the United States of America

1 2 3 4 5 6 7 8 9 10 09 08 07 06

CONTENTS

Cover picture: An air crash investigator photographs the wrecked cockpit of Pan Am Flight 103 on a hillside near Lockerbie, Scotland, on the morning after the December 22, 1988, disaster.

CHAPTER ONE

Pan Am Flight 103

The aim of terrorism is to spread terror. Terrorists seek to achieve their aims by using violence to make large numbers of people afraid enough to give in to their demands. Terrorist groups are usually small, and their actions, such as bombings and kidnappings, often have relatively few victims. Such acts, however, are planned to make whole societies or groups of people afraid of falling victim to similar attacks. Terrorists' aims vary: some want to create an independent state, for example, while others believe that they are acting from religious motives. Some terrorists operate on behalf of countries that fund, train, or shelter them. They operate secretly, enabling them to carry out attacks for which a country would be condemned in the international community. State-sponsored terrorists include the bombers of Pan Am Flight 103.

The Bombing

On December 21, 1988, Pan Am Flight 103 took off from London's Heathrow Airport headed for John F. Kennedy (JFK) Airport in New York City. There were two hundred and forty-three passengers on board, including twelve children. Of these, 189 were Americans heading home for the holidays. There were also sixteen crew members onboard. The flight was scheduled to leave Heathrow at 6:00 P.M., but a series of delays meant that the plane did not take off until 6:25 P.M.

Nearly forty minutes later, the plane had reached an altitude of 31,000 feet (9,450 m) and was on its way over Scotland. At 7:03 P.M., just as the plane was flying over the small village of Lockerbie, a small

▼ The cockpit of Pan Am Flight 103 lies in a field on a Scottish hillside after the aircraft was destroyed by a terrorist bomb on December 21, 1988.

bomb exploded in the cargo hold. Within seconds, the plane split apart and fell from the sky, hurtling to the ground at more than 200 miles (320 kilometers) per hour. The passengers and crew died almost instantly when the aircraft broke apart. As the wreckage of the airliner fell upon Lockerbie and the surrounding area, eleven people on the ground also died.

A total of two hundred and seventy people died as a result of the bombing of Flight Pan Am 103. More U.S. citizens were killed in the Pan Am 103 bombing than in any previous single incident in peacetime. The terrorist attacks of September 11, 2001, which killed around 2,800 Americans, would dwarf the number of people who died in the Pan Am disaster. At the time of the bombing, however, many Americans were shocked by the loss of so many fellow citizens. The disaster seemed even more tragic when it was revealed that the dead included a group of thirty-five students from

ATLANTIC OCEAN

SCOTLAND

Lockerbie

NORTHERN IRELAND

IRELAND

NORTH SEA

ENGLAND

WALES

THE NETHERLANDS

London

GERMANY

BELGIUM

Frankfurt

FRANCE

The Final Flight

Pan Am Flight 103 was a Boeing 747 named *Maid of the Seas*. It began its journey in Frankfurt, Germany, landing at Heathrow, in London, to take on more passengers for its flight to New York. The bomb blew up about forty minutes into the flight, above the village of Lockerbie.

Syracuse University who were on their way back from a semester abroad in Europe. The disaster also was the worst terrorist attack ever on British soil.

Scene of Tragedy

On the ground, the scene was one of devastation. One wing of the plane, complete with its nearly-full tank of fuel, and most of the fuselage, smashed a 150-foot (45-m) crater into a residential part of the village, destroying some houses completely and setting fire to others. The fireball caused by the exploding fuel could be seen 6 miles (9.5 km) away. The impact of the crash registered 1.6 on the Richter scale, which is used for measuring earthquakes. It was fortunate that falling debris did not kill

The Helsinki Warning

On December 5, 1988, two weeks before the Lockerbie disaster, a man with an Arabic accent, later identified as Yassan Garadet, telephoned the U.S. Embassy in Helsinki, Finland. The point of the phone call was to warn the U.S. government of a planned terrorist attack against an unnamed Pan Am flight leaving from Frankfurt within the next fourteen days.

This phone call has since become known as the Helsinki Warning. The warning was logged and recorded by staff at the embassy; it was also circulated among other embassy staff in Europe and passed on to Pan Am officials. Embassy and airline officials did not, however, consider the warning to be credible. U.S. airlines had often received threats, which always proved groundless. The phone call seemed like another in the long line of such threats.

Pan Am 103 fell from the sky sixteen days after the Helsinki warning, not the fourteen days specified in the warning. U.S. government officials say that the faulty timeline shows that the call was not a specific warning about the Lockerbie bomb. They say that it was a coincidence. Other people, including relatives of the victims, have since claimed that Pan Am's failure to increase security measures after the warning was irresponsible. They say that Pan Am did not take the warning seriously enough. Security staff at Frankfurt airport, where the flight began, only discovered the message about the Helsinki Warning the day after the Lockerbie bombing. It was buried under other papers on a desk.

even more people on the ground. Much of the wreckage fell in the open countryside outside of the village, including the cockpit, which landed in a field on a hillside.

A Routine Flight

The crash site came under the jurisdiction of John Boyd, chief constable of the Dumfries and Galloway region, in which Lockerbie is located. Boyd realized at once that the disaster was so big that it would require more resources than he had at his disposal. The constable used special emergency powers to call on military aid. Less than one hour after the crash, hundreds of British soldiers were on their way to Lockerbie to put out fires, to help survivors from the village, and to begin to retrieve the wreckage of the airplane and the bodies of the passengers and crew. Debris and bodies were scattered over a wide area toward Scotland's west coast. The search operation eventually extended over about 1,000 square miles (2,600 sq km) of the Scottish countryside.

In time, the soldiers and police officers were joined by specialized

Remembering The Victims

The victims of the bombing of Pan Am Flight 103 are remembered at Arlington National Cemetery, in Virginia, which is dedicated to national heroes. The village of Lockerbie sent the United States two hundred seventy blocks of sandstone—one for each victim. Frank Klein, a New Jersey builder whose daughter died in the disaster, used the stone to build a cairn, or stone tower, in the cemetery. The names of the dead are inscribed on its base.

In 1995, President Bill Clinton delivered a moving address at the site to mark the tenth anniversary of the bombing. He said, "None of us wants to live in a world where such violence goes unpunished and people can kill with impunity."

In recognition of the particular loss suffered by the community of Syracuse University, from which thirty-five students died, a trust fund was set up to allow high-school students from Lockerbie to benefit from a one-year scholarship to study at Syracuse. Students in the program study terrorism and its effects on global and local communities.

teams of experts from Britain and the United States. The British government sent officials from the Department of Transport's Air Accident Investigation Branch, while the U.S. government sent agents from the Federal Bureau of Investigation (FBI) and the Federal Aviation Administration (FAA). The British government established a Fatal Accident Inquiry to piece together the clues as to the cause of the incident. It was soon clear that the Lockerbie crash would require be one of the largest investigations of its kind in Britain.

Causes of the Crash

Flight 103 originated in Frankfurt, Germany. It had stopped in London to take on more passengers before heading north over Scotland and out over the Atlantic. Captain James

MacQuarrie and his copilot, Raymond Wagner, were both experienced pilots, and investigators soon decided that pilot error was highly unlikely to have caused the crash. A midair collision was equally unlikely, because air-traffic controllers reported that there had been no other aircraft in the vicinity.

Two likely explanations for the crash remained: Either the plane had suffered a mechanical malfunction or it had been blown up by an explosive device on board. Only careful examination of the debris would yield clues as to what had actually caused the disaster.

Piecing Together Clues

Chief Constable Boyd coordinated the search for evidence. Boyd took over an unused warehouse to store the various debris found by investigators. He split the warehouse into six separate areas. Each area corresponded to one of the six zones of the search area. As each piece of evidence was brought in from the various zones, it was tagged and placed in the corresponding section in the warehouse. The investigators were hoping that reconstructing the plane as best as they could would reveal the cause of the crash. They collected thousands of pieces of evidence, ranging from parts of the airplane to tiny pieces of passengers' possessions.

The first key piece of evidence was a fragment of a suitcase. The shape of the fragment, when placed together with a section of the fuselage, convinced investigators that a small bomb had exploded inside the suitcase. The suitcase had been in a container just 2 feet (60 cm) from the side of the forward section of the fuselage. The explosion had ripped apart the outer skin of the aircraft at the point of detonation and caused a shockwave that cracked the aircraft's frame just in front of the wings, making the plane split in half.

Over time, the reconstruction of the aircraft yielded more clues. Forensic scientists were able to find out more about the bomb that had caused the explosion. It had been made out of Semtex, a Czech-made plastic explosive favored by terrorists because it is powerful but also soft and easy to conceal. The Semtex had been hidden in a cassette player inside the suitcase.

Initial Suspects

The evidence was clear: Pan Am 103 had been the victim of a terrorist attack. But who were the terrorists? Investigators first looked to Iran and Syria, two Islamic countries in the Middle East. They based their suspicions on early forensic evidence, as well as on conflicts in the region.

Islamic countries in the Middle East were considered the mostly likely source of terrorism against the United States, partly because of strong U.S. support for Israel. The Islamic countries had long insisted that Palestine—the region where Israel had been created in the late 1940s—rightly belonged to Palestinian Arabs. For decades, many of the nations of the Middle East had sought the destruction of Israel.

The government of Iran, led by the religious leader Ayatollah Khomeni, was known to sponsor Hizb'allah, an anti-Israeli terrorist group based in Lebanon. Earlier in 1988, Hizb'allah had kidnapped and murdered U.S. Marine William Higgins in Lebanon.

Iran also had a specific grievance that might have motivated terrorist action against U.S. citizens. In July 1988, six months before the Lockerbie disaster, an Iranian passenger airliner

It was soon clear that the Lockerbie crash would require one of the largest investigations of its kind in Britain

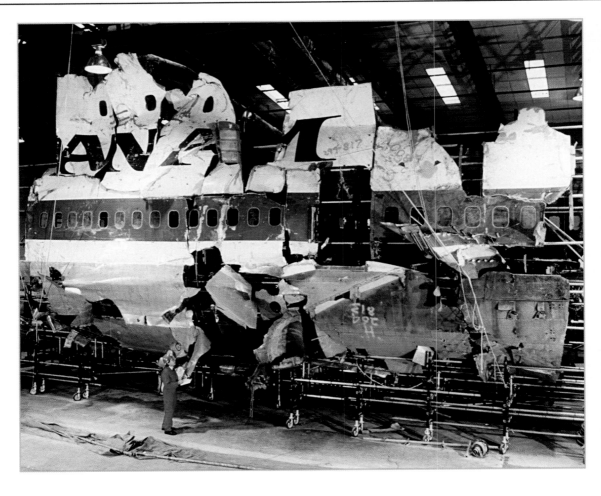

was shot down over the Persian Gulf by a missile fired from the U.S. warship USS *Vincennes*. Although the U.S. government claimed the incident was a mistake, it caused great anger in Iran. The country's leaders promised revenge against the United States.

Investigators knew that agents from Iran had visited Beirut, the capital of Lebanon. In Beirut, the Iranian agents had met with members of the Popular Front for the Liberation of Palestine— General Command (PLFP-GC), a terrorist group committed to destroying Israel and carrying out terror attacks against Israel's supporters.

▲ Air-accident investigators reconstructed parts of the airliner to help discover what had caused the crash.

The PLFP-GC was sponsored by the government of Syria.

Suspicions that the Iranians might have asked the PLFP-GC to bomb Pan Am 103 seemed to be confirmed when a PLFP-GC group was found in Germany making bombs hidden in cassette recorders. As the evidence mounted, however, investigators began looking to another Islamic state for the source of the bomb: the North African country of Libya.

A Tragic Mistake

Investigators originally thought the Lockerbie bombing may have been retaliation for the downing of an Iranian passenger plane by a U.S. naval ship. On July 3, 1988, Iran Air Flight 655 was shot down by the USS *Vincennes*. The warship was on patrol in the Persian Gulf to protect Kuwaiti oil tankers from attack by Iranian naval vessels. Flight 655 was on a scheduled flight to Dubai, but the crew of the *Vincennes* identified it as an Iranian military jet. Captain Will Rogers ordered a missile attack to destroy the plane. Two hundred and ninety passengers died on the aircraft, including sixty-three children.

After an investigation, the U.S. government apologized to the government of Iran and admitted that there had been a tragic mistake. It had been made worse by a series of circumstances. Flight 655 was twenty minutes late in taking off; the crew of the *Vincennes* believed the plane to be descending when it was ascending; and the pilots of the airliner did not reply to repeated requests from the *Vincennes* for identification. The requests, however, were sent on the wrong radio frequency.

Iran refused to accept the U.S. apology and swore vengeance on the United States and its citizens.

▼ The USS *Vincennes* fires a missile during drills after the September 11, 2001, attacks on the United States.

CHAPTER TWO

From Lockerbie to Libya

On December 28, 1988—one week after the Pan Am 103 disaster—Scottish police announced that the airplane had definitely been brought down by a bomb. The British Royal Armaments Research and Development Establishment (RARDE) confirmed that the bomb had been placed in a Toshiba cassette player. The evidence indicated that the cassette player had been placed in a brown Samsonite suitcase that was loaded into a baggage container situated near the front of the plane. RARDE officials pointed out that the bomb had been relatively small. Its location and the timing of the explosion—as the plane reached 31,000 feet—made its effect catastrophic.

Suspicion Falls on Iran

Armed with evidence that the destruction of Pan Am 103 had been caused by terrorist action, the police began to search for the culprits. All of the early evidence pointed to an Iranian or a Syrian connection. Just one day after the crash, an anonymous caller telephoned the offices of the Associated Press and United Press International to claim responsibility. The caller claimed that the Guardians of the Islamic Revolution had carried out the attack in revenge for the shooting down of the Iranian passenger aircraft by the USS *Vincennes*, and for the fact that the U.S. government had given refuge to the Shah, Iran's former ruler, after the 1979 Iranian Revolution. Although Western

▼ Libyan-sponsored terrorists blew up a French airliner in September 1989; the wreckage fell in the Sahara Desert.

counterterrorism experts knew little about the Guardians of the Islamic Revolution, the logic behind the attack seemed clear. The Iranian government had threatened "blood-splattered skies" in revenge for the deaths of its people in the *Vincennes* incident.

For Scottish police forces, the idea of a Middle Eastern connection to the attack seemed to be even more logical once they received information from German authorities about a recent operation in Frankfurt and elsewhere in Germany. In the months prior to the Pan Am disaster, German police officers had been watching a group of people of Middle Eastern descent suspected of plotting terrorist action on behalf of the Popular Front for the Liberation of Palestine—General Command (PFLP-GC).

On October 26, 1988, the police had arrested the leaders of the group. During a raid on their property, the police found evidence of attempts to make bombs. They even found a bomb built into a cassette player. The bomb's design suggested that it was intended to bring down an airplane because it was too small to do much damage

anywhere other than at a high altitude, where even a small hole in an airplane would almost certainly make it crash.

Security forces believed that it must be more than coincidence that German authorities in Frankfurt had discovered a bomb similar to the one that had brought down Pan Am 103, which had originated from Frankfurt. It seemed that the Frankfurt terrorists must be the bombers. Investigators set out to make a link between PFLP-GC terrorists in custody and the bombing.

The Palestinian Connection

The motive for the bombing fit investigators' suspicions. The PFLP-GC had broken away from the original Popular Front for the Liberation of Palestine (PFLP) because its members believed that the armed resistance against Israel had faltered. They believed that the PFLP did not launch enough attacks. The PFLP-GC was committed to a program of terrorist actions against Israel and its Western supporters, of whom the most important was the United States. Because Pan American Airlines was a U.S. airline, and because Pan Am 103 had been carrying mainly U.S. citizens, it seemed clear to Western security forces that the Lockerbie disaster was

▼ This scrap of clothing recovered by air crash investigators was wrapped around the cassette recorder containing the bomb. They traced the label to a small clothing store on the island of Malta.

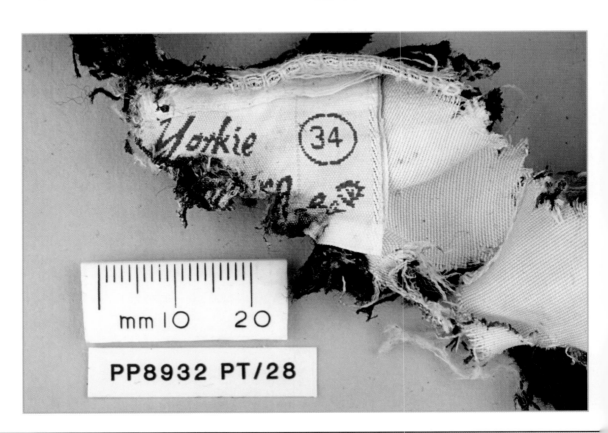

the work of the PFLP-GC. When they learned of the meeting between the PLFP-GC and representatives of the Iranian government just prior to the Lockerbie disaster, investigators reached what seemed to be the only possible conclusion: Pan Am Flight 103 had been brought down in revenge for the downing of Iran Air Flight 655, with the support of the Iranian government.

The Syrian Connection

In the year or so after the crash of Pan Am Flight 103, investigations centered upon the supposed Iranian connection. The investigation took another turn when it became clear that the PFLP-GC was largely funded by the government of Syria. The possibility now arose that Iranian leaders had "subcontracted" the terrorist act to the Syrian-backed PFLP-GC. In fact, relations between Syria and Western governments, particularly the United States, had deteriorated to such an extent throughout the 1980s that some Western analysts believed it possible that the Syrian government might have carried out the operation on its own, using the PFLP-GC to strike against the United States, the main Western supporter of Israel.

A New Theory

Investigators in Scotland, however, kept returning to the bomb itself and also to the other contents of the suitcase that had contained it. As time went on, explosives experts became more convinced that the bomb had not originated in Frankfurt, as had first been thought.

Investigators found a fragment of a shirt that had been blown apart and burned in a way that suggested that it had been wrapped around the cassette player. Part of the label of the shirt was visible. When investigators analyzed it, they concluded that the shirt had come from a store called Mary's House, which was located in the seaside town of Sliema on the Mediterranean island of Malta. When investigators interviewed the owner of the store, Tony Gauci, he remembered selling the shirt and other clothing. He said he had noticed the customer who bought them because he appeared to be buying clothes at random. Gauci also described the buyer of the shirt as being of North African appearance.

The Libya Link

As the investigation of the Maltese connection continued, evidence of the involvement of Libya began to grow. Geographically, Malta is close to Libya. Libyan intelligence agents had a long history of operating on the island, and they had a strong presence at Malta's Luqa International Airport, where the Lockerbie bomb was now thought to have originated.

Libya's ruler, Colonel Muammar Muhammad al-Gadhafi, had declared himself to be an enemy of Israel and its Western supporters from the time he had taken power in 1969. Gadhafi was also known to have aided various terrorist groups in Western countries, most notably the Irish Republican Army (IRA) in Northern Ireland, which had waged a long terrorist campaign against the British government.

Gadhafi was also strongly suspected of having authorized the September 1989 bombing of a French DC-10 airliner, Flight UTA 772, flying out of Brazzaville in the Congo, which exploded in midair, killing all one hundred and seventy passengers and crew members. In October 1991, a French magistrate issued warrants for the arrest of four Libyan officials accused of masterminding the blast; the warrant said that the bomb had been placed on the airplane by Congolese terrorists recruited by the Libyans. Libya had previously attacked French targets because of France's support for the government of Chad against rebel insurgents; Gadhafi had backed the rebels in the hopes of getting access to the rich resources of northern Chad.

Libya and Terrorism

Western governments had already accused Libya of sponsoring terrorism. Gadhafi used the country's wealth from its oil wells to support groups in what he saw as Arab nationalist causes—such as attacks on Israel and its supporters—and anti-imperialist causes, including attacks on Western powers who were economically influential in North Africa.

In April 1986, U.S. president Ronald Reagan authorized air strikes on Libya's capital, Tripoli, in retaliation for what Reagan said was "irrefutable" evidence of Libyan involvement in the blowing up of a discotheque in Berlin, Germany. The disco was popular among U.S. servicemen, one of whom was among the two people killed in the blast. The air strike missed Gadhafi but killed his adopted daughter, Hannah. After the attack, Gadhafi swore revenge against the United States and its allies. He also took care to operate more secretly. In the past, terrorist activities had been coordinated through Libyan People's Bureaus, or embassies. After the attack, Gadhafi worked through other groups to avoid being blamed for attacks.

The U.S. government believed, for example, that Gadhafi funded numerous terrorist groups to make strikes to mark the second and third anniversaries of the bombing raid on Tripoli. In April 1988, an anarchist group called the Japanese Red Army bombed a nightclub in Naples, Italy, killing five people including a U.S. servicewoman. Over the next five days, U.S. targets were bombed in Spain, Colombia, Peru, and Costa Rica. In

> **Gadhafi was also known to have aided various terrorist groups in other Western countries, most notably the Irish Republican Army (IRA)**

April 1989, the Tupac Amaru (MRTA) group in Peru again tried to bomb the United States Information Service (USIS) office in Lima, Peru's capital.

▲ This crater was made by a missile during U.S. air raids on the Libyan capital of Tripoli in April 1986. Dozens of Libyans died in the raids, possibly providing a motive for Libya's bombing of Pan Am Flight 103.

Forms of Sponsorship

Libya's sponsorship of terrorism took numerous forms, including direct funding for groups, providing advice and coordination, and harboring terrorist training camps. The national airline, Libyan Arab Airlines, transported terrorists to and from operations, while Libyan companies provided a front for weapons smuggling and intelligence gathering.

Much of Libya's support went to groups that supported the Palestinian terrorist campaigns against Israel, such as Palestinian Islamic Jihad and the PFLP-GC, the group originally thought to be involved in the Pan Am bombing. The sums involved were sometimes high: In 1990 alone, the PFLP-GC received $1 million. Libya's sponsorship of terrorism, however, went far beyond the Middle East. Its Anti-Imperialism Center coordinated funds, advice, arms, and training for groups operating as far afield as Europe, Africa, Latin America—including Colombia, Peru, Chile, Costa Rica, and Haiti—and the Pacific. In the Philippines, the New People's Army, which was associated with the Communist Party, received $7 million from Libya between 1987 and 1991. Within Libya, training camps were established for terrorists from different organizations. Groups from Africa and Latin America trained at the Seven April and Bin Ghashir camps. The Ras al-Hilal camp was for Palestinian terrorists, while the anti-Israel Abu Nidal Organization (ANO) trained at the al-Qalah camp.

The ANO carried out some of the highest profile attacks linked with Libya before the Lockerbie bombing. In November 1987, it hijacked a yacht in the Mediterranean and took five French and Belgian passengers hostage. These hostages were not all released until 1991. In July 1988, the ANO hijacked the Greek cruise ship *City of Poros* near Athens with machine guns and grenades. Nine passengers died and more than a hundred were injured in the attack.

Two New Suspects

In October 1990, nearly two years after the bombing of Pan Am 103,

many observers were surprised when claims appeared in the Western media that Libya, rather than Iran or Syria, might have been behind the Lockerbie disaster. Newspapers in France and the United States reported that the timer used in the explosion was identical to timers found in the possession of two Libyan intelligence agents arrested in Senegal ten months before the Pan Am bombing. By the end of the year, investigators knew that the timer came from a Swiss manufacturing company that Libyan intelligence agents had used in the past.

After further investigation, the investigators narrowed their focus to two suspects, both of whom had motive and opportunity to plant the bomb: Abdel Basset Al-Megrahi and Lamin Khalifa Fhimah. Al-Megrahi was head of airline security for the Libyan intelligence service, Jamahirya Security Organization (JSO), where he had worked under the two Libyans arrested in Senegal; Fhimah worked for Libyan Arab Airlines (LAA) at Luqa Airport in Malta.

Following the Clues

Nearly two years after the bombing of Pan Am 103, the investigators had completed their work. Their remarkable forensic investigation led

> **Many observers were surprised when claims appeared in the Western media that Libya might have been behind the Lockerbie disaster.**

The Career of a Terrorist

One of the most notorious terrorist groups sheltered by Libya was the Abu Nidal Organization (ANO), named for its Syrian leader, Abu Nidal, who was also known as Sabri al-Banna. As a result of warnings before the bombing of Flight 103, Abu Nidal was for a time the chief suspect.

Nidal built up the ANO after leaving the Palestine Liberation Organization (PLO) in 1974 and attacked targets he associated with support for Israel. In December 1985, for example, the ANO said it carried out machine-gun attacks on passengers at Rome and Vienna airports in which nine people died and 100 were injured.

Nidal had received funding from Libya in the 1970s, and, in 1987, he moved his base to Libya from Syria. ANO terrorists trained at the al-Qalah camp near Tripoli—they received Libyan passports—while Nidal himself lived in the capital. He also enjoyed the protection of Syria and was able to travel freely throughout the Middle East with little fear of arrest.

In 1988, German security forces believed they thwarted an attempt by the ANO to attack U.S. targets in Germany. In the late 1980s, the ANO began to suffer internal wrangles and Nidal and his associates probably killed many of their own members. Nidal's terrorist activities tapered off in the 1990s. In 2002, he was found dead in Iraq. One of his followers later claimed that Nidal had been responsible for the Lockerbie bombing.

◀ Abu Nidal was one of the world's most notorious terrorists. In 2002, he died under mysterious circumstances in Iraq.

them to conclude that agents of the Libyan intelligence service had carried out the attack. Because Gadhafi was involved in every aspect of Libya's state-sponsored terrorism, they alleged that he must have personally ordered the attack.

Investigators believed the two men had planted a bomb at Luqa Airport that was transferred to Pan Am Flight 103 in Frankfurt. Investigators discovered from airline records that

Al-Megrahi had traveled to Malta on December 7, 1988. On Malta, he bought clothes at Mary's House, the owner of which later identified him from photographs. A few days later, Magrihi and Fhimah traveled to Libya. On December 20, they returned to Malta with a Samsonite suitcase. They put the cassette player containing the bomb into the case, along with the clothes bought at Mary's House.

Fhimah then used his role as LAA station manager at Luqa Airport to avoid security checks and insert the suitcase among the baggage headed for Frankfurt on Air Malta Flight KM 180. Fhimah attached stolen Pan Am tags to the case to make sure that it would be transferred in Frankfurt onto the flight to New York via London.

▲ Libyan leader Colonel Gadhafi (right) joins demonstrations in August 1998 against U.S. air attacks on suspected terrorist targets in Sudan and Afghanistan.

Bringing Charges

On November 14, 1991, the Scottish Crown Office and the U.S. State Department announced simultaneous indictments against the two chief suspects. On the same day, British home secretary Douglas Hurd told the House of Commons that the British government was satisfied that no other country was involved in the Lockerbie bombing. President George H. W. Bush said that Syria had taken "a bum rap" for the bombing. As far as the British and U.S. governments were concerned,

▲ This courtroom sketch shows the Scottish courtroom set up at Camp Zeist in the Netherlands. The trials of al-Megrahi and Fhima followed Scottish law.

the Lockerbie bombing was a Libyan government action from beginning to end.

Arranging a Trial

The British and American governments called on Libya to extradite the two accused agents, so they could stand trial in Great Britain. Gadhafi, however, refused to turn the men over, claiming that they would never receive a fair trial in a British court of law. Britain and the United States responded by declaring Libya to be a "pariah," or outlaw, state. Under pressure from the United States, the United Nations (UN), an organization of countries established to promote peace and mediate disputes among nations, voted to impose sanctions on Libya. The sanctions meant that Libya would not be able to trade in certain goods with UN members until Gadhafi handed the agents over for trial and publicly renounced his sponsorship of international terrorism. The sanctions severely damaged Libya's international trade and its economy.

Meanwhile, the families of the

Libya's IRA Connections

During the 1980s, Colonel Gadhafi turned Libya into a haven for terrorists who would strike against countries he saw as imperialist powers or supporters of Israel. Gadhafi established camps where his security forces trained terrorist groups such as Euskadi Ta Akatasuna (ETA), which sought the independence of the Basque region in Spain, and Corsicans and Bretons in conflict with the French government. Other visitors included anti-government Colombian rebels; the Red Brigades, from Italy; and the Sandanistas, from Nicaragua. Gadhafi also extended his invitation to the Irish Republican Army (IRA), which was fighting against British rule in Northern Ireland. IRA members enthusiastically took advantage of the offer.

Libya served as a major supplier of arms for the IRA throughout the 1980s. These weapons allowed the terrorists to carry out such attacks as the bombing of Enniskillen on Remembrance Sunday (Veterans' Day) in 1987. This blast killed eleven people and injured 63. In 1991, the IRA used mortar bombs from Libya to bomb 10 Downing Street, the official residence of the British prime minister, during a Cabinet meeting chaired by Prime Minister John Major.

This attack led to greater efforts by British security forces to break the close links between Libya and the IRA. British authorities reasoned that, if its supply line of arms and ammunition could be severed, the IRA would be dealt a major blow. They used improved intelligence-gathering and surveillance techniques. The result was a remarkable run of success for the authorities in detecting and intercepting these arms shipments, virtually stopping them completely.

Perhaps the most famous of these interceptions, because of the sheer size of the illegal arms cache found, was the seizing of the merchant ship *Eksund* in 1987. It was captured as it tried to deliver 150 tons of Libyan arms to the IRA.

▼ In 1987, the IRA used explosives supplied by Libya to bomb a Remembrance Sunday parade in Enniskillen, killing eleven people.

victims who had died on Pan Am 103 had organized themselves into pressure groups in both the United States and Britain. They launched a campaign of letter-writing and protests in order to put pressure on Gadhafi and the Libyan regime. A stalemate ensued.

In November 1993, the UN Security Council passed Resolution 883, which further tightened sanctions against Libya by restricting its oil industry. The sanctions were beginning to take their toll in Libya. It seemed that the United States and Britain were determined to use Libya's refusal to hand over the suspected terrorists as a way to bring about Gadhafi's fall from power.

The next day they were formally accused of conspiracy to commit two hundred and seventy acts of murder

A Trial At Last

In 1998, Gadhafi finally gave in to the pressure on the Libyan economy and agreed to turn al-Megrahi and Fhimah over for trial. Under a complex legal arrangement set up to answer Libya's concerns that the men would not receive a fair trial in Great Britain, a special court was set up in the Netherlands. It was staffed by Scottish judges and lawyers and operated according to Scottish law. On April 5, 1999, the two men arrived in the Netherlands to be arrested. The next day they were formally accused of conspiracy to commit 270 acts of murder.

The Verdict

In spite of the forensic case the crash investigators had built, many legal experts believed that the material evidence linking the two men to the bombing was slim. The store owner in Malta, for example, was not completely certain about his identification of al-Megrahi. However, on January 31, 2001, the three Scottish judges announced that Abdel Basset Al-Megrahi was guilty on all counts; Lamin Khalifa Fhimah, on the other hand, was acquitted.

Al-Megrahi was sentenced to life imprisonment, with the condition that he serve at least twenty years in prison. He is currently serving his sentence in a Scottish prison. Just over twelve years after the bombing, it appeared that the culprit had finally been brought to justice. However, the lack of hard evidence still left doubt in the minds of some observers. Martin Cadman, the father of a British victim of the bombing, said, "Before the trial started, I had taken the view that it was going to be a farce. And nothing that has happened since has changed that."

Unanswered Questions

Numerous conspiracy theories evolved about unanswered questions about the bombing. Some people, for example,

Conspiracy Theories

Almost as soon as Al-Megrahi was found guilty, analysts and some of the victims' relatives denounced the verdict as part of a conspiracy. Conspiracy theorists contend that the British and U.S. governments covered up links between the bombing and the PFLP-GC and its Iranian and Syrian sponsors.

One theory says that the PFLP-GC planted the bomb on behalf of Iran in revenge for the downing of Iran Air Flight 655 by the U.S. Navy in 1988. A variation on the theory claims that PFLP-GC leader Ahmed Jibril took orders directly from the Syrian government. A twist on this theory, which first surfaced in *Time* magazine in the early 1990s, argues that the PFLP-GC was able to smuggle the bomb onto the airplane because security was kept lax so that U.S. Drug Enforcement Administration (DEA)

agents could use Pan Am Flight 103 to ship drugs from the Middle East into Europe. According to the theory, the DEA allowed the drugs to be transported in return for intelligence from Middle-East sources about U.S. hostages held in Lebanon.

The conspiracy theorists share a common belief: the United States did not want to alienate Syria or Iran, which had influence over terrorist groups holding U.S. hostages. After the Persian Gulf War in 1991, meanwhile, Britain and the U.S. needed political and strategic allies in the Middle East. According to the conspiracy theories, both governments wanted to play down Syrian or Iranian involvement in the bombing. Libya, already politically isolated, was a convenient scapegoat.

speculated that the implication of Libya in the crime in the first place reflected the political situation in the years after the bombing more than the evidence. The United States, they believe, did not want to blame Syria for the bombing, because it needed Syrian government help to negotiate with Syrian-backed terrorists who had taken U.S. hostages in the Middle East.

Conspiracy theories about the case gained more momentum when al-Megrahi lost an appeal in June 2002.

Despite admitting doubts over the lack of direct evidence linking Al-Megrahi to the bomb, the Scottish appeals court upheld the verdict.

Gadhafi meanwhile accepted the verdict and said that Libya would pay compensation to the victims of the Lockerbie bombing of $10 million per passenger; so far, Libya has paid out almost $2.5 billion in compensation. Gadhafi also agreed to give up his weapons of mass destruction and publicly stated his intention to end Libyan sponsorship of terrorism.

Jim Swire: Tireless Campaigner

For many people, the public face of the grief, anger, and frustration felt by the relatives of the victims of the Pan Am bombing was best represented by British doctor Jim Swire. Swire and his wife, Jane, had lost their 23-year-old daughter Flora on the flight. Like other relatives of the victims, Swire was determined to get to the bottom of who had carried out the bombing. He proved to be most uncommon, however, in the energy, perseverance, and doggedness with which he campaigned for the truth.

Swire became spokesperson for the British victims' group, UK Families—Flight 103. In 1989, he tried to persuade the British government to set up a formal inquiry to discover the truth about the crash. When the government rejected the idea, Swire went to court to try to force British prime minister Margaret Thatcher and Paul Channon, the former transportation secretary, to testify at the Fatal Accident Inquiry. The politicians invoked laws that allow members of Parliament to avoid giving evidence in court.

Swire engaged in a long letter-writing campaign, corresponding with government ministers, other victims' relatives, and the media. His aim was two-fold: to find out the truth and to keep alive public interest in the Lockerbie bombing.

Swire was also concerned about continuing problems with flight safety. He once successfully smuggled a fake bomb onto an airliner in order to expose the lax security still in place at British airports.

As negotiations related to the trial of the Libyan suspects dragged on, Swire even went to Libya to try to persuade Colonel Gadhafi to hand them over. This move made Swire unpopular among many of the other victims' relatives who thought that it might endanger the long diplomatic negotiations about the trial.

▼ At a news conference in February 2001, Jim Swire displays an image of a detonator similar to the one used to set off the bomb on Pan Am 103.

CHAPTER THREE

State-Sponsored Terrorism

State-sponsored terrorism has a long history. Leaders have used terror against opponents within their own states or against potential enemies in other lands. In the late fourteenth century, the Mongol warrior Timur the Lame massacred whole cities on his campaigns of conquest in Central and West Asia. He wanted his terrifying reputation to spread to other cities to make people more reluctant to resist his armies. In the twentieth century, Soviet leader Joseph Stalin used terror to make sure he had no rivals for power. He regularly purged, or eliminated, high-ranking politicians in the Soviet Union. Some of them were killed by the secret police; others were subjected to public "show trials," which were phony trials staged to discourage opposition to Stalin.

In these cases, leaders used their own forces to carry out terrorism. But governments have also used terrorist groups that cannot easily be linked to them. When these groups attack foreign targets, it is often difficult to trace their actions back to the governments that assisted them.

Helping Terrorists

Terrorist groups that receive assistance from governments can be a particular threat to peace. The resources of even a poor country are almost always far greater than those of any terrorist organization. Countries can provide large amounts of cash and provide safe bases and freedom from investigation by

▼ Members of the Kurdish Workers' Party, an anti-Turkish terror group, display their weapons at their training camp in Syria.

authorities. They can also supply arms and sophisticated military hardware. They can give terrorists access to broad intelligence-gathering networks and provide logistical support, such as false documentation or transportation on national airlines.

Terrorist weapons are sometimes smuggled in diplomatic bags, which are privileged packages sent between governments and their embassies that are not searched in the same way as normal international mail. A state can also use its embassy in another country, which is protected from the host country's laws, to shelter terrorists. In 1986, for example, British authorities discovered that a Syrian terrorist had plotted to plant a bomb on an aircraft in London, but he took refuge in Syria's embassy in London.

Fighting state-sponsored terrorism is also highly difficult. Governments have the right to act as they wish in their own countries. States can refuse to extradite, or hand over to another country for trial, suspected terrorists, as Libya initially did with the two men suspected of the bombing of Pan Am Flight 103.

▲ These bombs packed into blue canisters were found by Syrian police, along with guns and other weapons, after a terrorist attack in 2004. Syria may have become a target for terrorists after it reduced its own support for their activities.

What Is Terrorism?

It is sometimes difficult to clarify exactly what is state-sponsored terrorism and what is not. Some acts of violence and illegal killing carried out by governments or sponsored by them are not strictly terrorism, because they are not intended to spread terror. These acts can include examples where governments have practiced genocide to try to wipe out portions of their populations. From 1975 to 1979, for example, the Khmer Rouge government of Cambodia murdered a million of its own citizens to stay in power. In Iraq, in 1988, dictator Saddam Hussein launched poison gas attacks against Iraq's Kurdish population. Although the attacks did have the effect of spreading fear throughout large communities of people, terrorism was not their principle aim.

In other cases, actions that are intended to spread fear are carried out not by traditional terrorist groups, which tend to be small and secret, but by the agencies of the state themselves. These agencies include Stalin's notorious secret police, the NKVD, as well as the Waffen-SS troops in Nazi Germany. The Waffen-SS were responsible for carrying out the Holocaust, the murder of six million Jews and millions of other people in concentration camps. During World War II (1939–1945), the SS were also responsible for committing atrocities against civilians in Russia that were intended to terrify Russians into not resisting the German occupation.

Governments sometimes use violence and terror tactics against their own people if they believe it is necessary for the preservation of the state. Such was the case with the crackdown by the Chinese government against protestors gathered in Tiananmen Square in June 1989 to protest the strict communist government in Beijing. The crowd grew over weeks until, on June 4, 1989, the government sent in troops to clear the square. Hundreds of people died in the operation, and thousands were later tried and imprisoned. Chinese leaders were concerned that the demonstrations represented a threat to the existence of the state. For this reason, in spite of outrage around the world, they believed their use of force against the protestors was justified.

Supporters of Terrorism

Most democratic nations avoid direct contact with organizations that are clearly terrorist groups. The governments most closely associated with sponsoring terrorism tend to be those that are dictatorships or one-party states. They tend to reject open government, legal procedure, and human rights, and their actions are not open to judicial review. Working with terror groups allows them to deny responsibility for an act in the international community. It also tends to be cheaper than using armed forces, and makes it easier for them to act secretly.

In the second half of the twentieth century the most common sponsors of terrorism were radical states in the Middle East—particularly Libya, Iran, Syria, and Iraq—and communist states, including the Soviet Union and its eastern European satellites, North Korea, and Cuba.

Like Libya, the other Middle Eastern states were motivated to sponsor terrorism partly by their opposition to the existence of Israel in a region that they claim belongs to the Arab Palestinians. States such as Iran were also motivated by Islamism, the desire to establish Islamic governments and to attack perceived enemies of Islamic values, such as the United States and other Western nations. Communist states, on the other hand, saw terrorist acts as a means to advance the communist revolution against countries using the capitalist economic system.

Other countries that have been accused of sponsoring terrorism include Pakistan, South Africa, and Israel. During the Apartheid era (1948–1992), for example, South Africa funded terrorist groups to destabilize neighboring countries that were hostile to its government. The groups included the RENAMO, which carried out atrocities on civilians in Mozambique to destabilize the country's left-wing government.

In its struggle against Palestinian terrorist groups, meanwhile, Israel provided arms and training to local militias, including the Phalange, a right-wing Christian group in largely Islamic Lebanon. In 1975, this group massacred a busload of Palestinians, triggering civil war in Lebanon

The most common sponsors of terrorism were radical states in the Middle East—particularly Libya, Iran, Syria, and Iraq

between Islamic and Christian forces. In 1982, the Phalange took part in the massacre of hundreds of Palestinians in two refugee camps near Beirut, Sabra and Chatila.

Communism and Terrorism

The sponsorship of terrorism by communist states was particularly common during the Cold War, the rivalry between the United States and its Western allies and the Soviet Union

> **In 1990, Iran hosted a "World Conference on Palestine," attended by all the leading Palestinian terrorist groups**

and its communist allies that lasted from about 1945 until 1989. While the two superpowers tried to avoid direct confrontation, the communist nations turned to supporting terrorist groups.

U.S. analysts believed that the Soviet Union sponsored terrorists in Europe, the Middle East, and Latin America to destabilize governments sympathetic to the United States and its allies. The extent of such sponsorship remains uncertain. After the reunification of Germany in 1990, however, records released by the East German secret police, the Stasi, showed that communist East Germany had financed terrorist groups in Europe in the 1970s and 1980s. These groups included the Red Army Faction, also known as the Baader-Meinhof Gang. The group attacked targets associated with West Germany and its allies to protest capitalism. It also conducted a campaign of bombings, kidnappings,

and assassinations, and joined Palestinian terrorists in high-profile hijackings of airliners.

In Asia, communist North Korea has maintained a bitter struggle against neighboring South Korea. Its intelligence agencies have acted almost in the same way as terrorists, launching covert operations such as the one in 1983 in which commandos blew up the South Korean cabinet. North Korea also provided arms to the New People's Army in the Philippines, the military branch of the Filipino Communist Party, which waged a terrorist campaign in rural areas.

Iran and Terrorism

After the government of the Shah in Iran fell in 1979 and was replaced by an Islamic People's Republic, the new government made terrorism a central policy of the state. It sent Iranian agents to assassinate opposition figures abroad. In 1991, for example, one of its agents killed former Iranian prime minister Shahpur Bakhtiar in Paris.

Iran also sponsored Islamic terrorist groups as part of what it saw as its role in leading a worldwide Islamic revolution. The groups it sponsored include the Supreme Council of the Islamic Revolution, in Iraq; Hizb'allah, in Lebanon; and Palestinian Islamic Jihad. Hizb'allah, for example, received

State-Sponsored Terrorism in History

Governments have sometimes tried to silence opposition by terrorizing their own people. One of the most infamous examples of this occurred during the French Revolution in the late eighteenth century. A series of rapidly changing governments rose to power and executed their predecessors and any potential opponents to try to consolidate their own power. The condemned were tried by revolutionary courts and executed by guillotine. From 1793 to 1794, at the height of what became known as the Reign of Terror, about thirty thousand people were killed.

Another notorious use of terror occurred in the Soviet Union from the 1930s to the 1950s. Russian leader Joseph Stalin wiped out former colleagues and anyone suspected of "counter-revolutionary" activities. The precise number of victims of Stalin's terror is still uncertain because he operated secretly; some Russian historians estimate the total to be around seven million. Stalin's victims were arrested by the notorious secret police and tortured into giving names of other counter-revolutionaries before they were shot. Stalin also staged "show trials" in which defendants were forced to admit publicly to their "crimes." Those found guilty were either shot or sent to harsh labor camps, where many more died.

▼ Among the first victims of the Reign of Terror was King Louis XVI, who was killed in January 1793. The executions during the Terror were public spectacles intended to spread fear in the public.

funding of up to $80 million a year for its operations in Lebanon in the 1980s, and military and diplomatic support. Hizb'allah bombed U.S. embassies and other locations and kidnapped and sometimes murdered western hostages. In 1990, Iran hosted a "World Conference on Palestine," attended by representatives from all the leading Palestinian terrorist groups.

Iran also sponsored groups to attack states in the Arab Gulf dominated by the Sunni branch of Islam. Most people in Iran follow the Shiite branch of the faith, and bitter hostility exists between the two groups. Iran trained Shiite Kuwaitis to sabotage Kuwait's economy by bombing oil installations. Their other actions included the hijacking of an airliner in 1987 to try to force Kuwait to release imprisoned terrorists. The hijackers ordered the airliner to fly to Iran, where Kuwaiti authorities believed that Iran helped the hijackers to escape.

Another target for Iranian-sponsored terrorism was Sunni Saudi Arabia. In 1989, Kuwaitis trained by Iran bombed people making the *hajj*, the annual Muslim pilgrimage to the holy city of Mecca. Other groups assassinated Saudi diplomats in Lebanon and Pakistan.

Iraq and Terrorism

While Iran sponsored terrorism, it was also a target of terror attacks sponsored by its neighbor and enemy, Iraq. Before the Iraqi government of Saddam Hussein fell in 2003 after the invasion by the United States and its allies, it sponsored the Iranian Mujahedin-e Khalq Organization (MKO) to oppose

▼ Al-Qaeda terrorists train at a camp in Afghanistan in October 2001. A U.S.-led coalition invaded Afghanistan to destroy al-Qaeda after the attacks of September 11.

Iran's fundamentalist Shiite government. The organization had a political wing in Paris, France, and conventional armed forces based in Iraq, but it also had terrorist cells operating within Iran. It is not clear how strong the organization was in Iran, where the authorities took harsh measures against suspected members. In June 1994, however, an MKO bomb in the city of Masshad killed 25 people and injured many more.

Other Iraqi-sponsored terrorism included attacks on foreign workers in northern Iraq—the government offered killers a reward for each foreigner who died—and a 1993 plot to kill U.S. president George H. W. Bush with a car bomb while he was on a visit to Kuwait after the Persian Gulf War.

They said that they had been trained in bombing, shooting, and even beheading

The plot was discovered and six Iraqis and Kuwaitis were later executed for their part in the operation.

Hussein also used terror tactics against his own people to extinguish any opposition to his rule. Iraq's infamous intelligence agency, the Mukhabarat, assassinated Saddam's critics both inside and outside Iraq. It also detained tens of thousands of ordinary Iraqis suspected of any form of dissent, torturing them and holding them in crowded cells without trial, often for years. When U.S.-led forces overthrew Saddam's government in 2003, they found mass graves of people executed by the Mukhabarat.

Syria and Terrorism

The Syrian military government of Hafiz al-Assad, who was president of the country from 1971 to 2000, sponsored terror groups to carry out attacks linked to Syrian objectives, particularly the destabilization of Israel. Even before Assad came to power, Syria sponsored Fatah, the most powerful of the parties that made up the Palestine Liberation Organization (PLO). Syria trained and armed Fatah in order to wage a terrorist campaign inside Israel. The Popular Front for the Liberation of Palestine-General Command (PFLP-GC), which some people still believe was closely linked to the Lockerbie bombing, was another Syrian-backed group that launched attacks on targets within Israel. The extremist anti-Israeli Abu Nidal Organization was also based in Syria before it relocated to Libya.

In the 1980s and 1990s, during which time Syrian troops occupied most of Lebanon, the country became the base for a range of terrorist groups. They included the Kurdish Workers' Party, a Marxist group that launches attacks against Turkish targets, seeking independence from Turkey. At the same time, Syria sought to destabilize Turkey, because the countries were in dispute about water rights on the region's rivers. Other anti-Turkish

The United States as a Sponsor of Terrorism

Some Western democracies, such as the United States and Great Britain, have been accused by other governments, human rights organizations, or political opponents of supporting terrorism or of turning a blind eye to other countries' involvement in terrorism. In the 1980s, for example, the U.S. government funded the Contras, a rebel group fighting the government in Nicaragua. The Contras engaged in illegal acts, attacking government-related targets and murdering, torturing, or robbing Nicaraguans who did not back them. They and the U.S. administration, however, argued that they were rebel fighters rather than terrorists, claiming that their primary aim was to wage a guerrilla war rather than to spread terror.

In other Latin American countries, such as Colombia, the United States supported governments that were suspected of using death squads against their opponents. The U.S. government argued that military assistance was a vital part of its war on drugs in Colombia and that no proof linked other governments to the death squads.

◀ Contra fighters salute during a speech by one of their commanders. The U.S. administration argued that the Contras were rebels rather than terrorists.

terrorist groups supported by Syria in Lebanon are the Armenian Secret Army for the Liberation of Armenia (ASALA) and the Revolutionary Left (Dev Sol). In 1991, Dev Sol bombed more than thirty Western-related targets in Turkey. Three years later, it assassinated a former justice minister, Mehmet Topac.

After Hafiz al-Assad died in 2000, his son Bashar became president of Syria. International observers believed that Bashar would cut Syria's ties with terrorism. In 2005, however, Syria was implicated in the assassination of Rafik Hariri, the former prime minister of Lebanon. The popular demonstrations that resulted in Lebanon eventually forced Syria to announce that it would withdraw its military forces from Lebanon, which it had effectively occupied for 29 years.

In February 2005, captured terrorists who had taken part in the insurgency

Terrorism in South Asia

In August 1947, Britain granted independence to India. British India was divided into two separate countries, each with its own religion. India became a mostly Hindu state, while Pakistan became a Muslim state. After partition, as the division of the country was known, the mountainous border region of Kashmir was disputed between the two.

After a series of inconclusive wars to resolve possession of Kashmir, successive Pakistani governments resorted to terrorism to achieve their goals. India has accused Pakistan of facilitating the infiltration of terrorists across the heavily-armed frontier, in an attempt to destabilize the Indian-controlled part of Kashmir. It suspects Pakistan of financing, arming, and training the Hizbul Mujahideen and the Jammu and Kashmir Liberation Front (JKLF) to achieve this goal.

Pakistan-controlled terrorists have also carried out bombings and assassinations in in India itself, including a double explosion in the Indian city of Mumbai (Bombay) in 2004 that killed at least fifty people.

India itself supported the terrorist Tamil Tigers from 1983 to 1987 in their separatist war against the government of Sri Lanka. After the Indian government withdrew its support, it sent forces to Sri Lanka to help halt the Tigers' terror campaign. In 1991, the Tigers assassinated former Indian prime minister Rajiv Gandhi in retaliation.

against the U.S.-led occupation of Iraq claimed that they had been financed by Syria. They said that they had been trained in bombing, shooting, and even beheading, and that their campaign was meant "to cause chaos in Iraq to bar America from reaching Syria." Syria denied their claim.

Afghanistan and Terrorism

In Afghanistan, the Soviet-backed government fell in 1989 after a long struggle with Islamic guerrilla fighters. One of the groups of warriors, the Taliban ("God's students"), eventually came to rule the country. They were extreme fundamentalists who imposed strict Islamic rule on Afghanistan. The Taliban also sought to promote what it saw as an Islamic revolution, and it allowed Islamist terrorist groups to train their volunteers in the use of arms, in terror tactics, and in guerrilla warfare. The Taliban offered a haven for the Saudi-born Osama bin Laden, leader of the terrorist group al-Qaeda, after he was expelled from Sudan for his links with terrorism in 1996. Bin Laden shared the Taliban's religious views. After al-Qaeda's September 11, 2001, attacks on New York City and Washington, D. C., the United States led an invasion of Afghanistan that brought down the Taliban government.

CHAPTER FOUR

Responses to State-Sponsored Terrorism

Responding to state-sponsored terrorism can be very difficult. Even if a link between a terrorist group and its sponsor is certain—and such a link is often difficult to prove—other countries have few legal options available apart from imposing economic sanctions or declaring war. In the case of a government supporting or carrying out terrorist acts within its own borders, other governments again have few options. In most cases, other countries are powerless to prevent a nation from doing what it wants within its own borders.

Security Checks

One of the main responses to terrorism—including state-sponsored terrorism—is to try to prevent future acts. Even before the bombing of Pan Am Flight 103, a series

▼ U.S. Marines march out toward the front line near Kandahar in Afghanistan in December 2001, during Operation Enduring Freedom. The U.S.-led action brought down the Taliban government that had sheltered al-Qaeda and destroyed al-Qaeda's bases, but it failed to capture the terrorists' leaders, who may have fled to Pakistan.

of airline attacks had led to greater security at airports. These attacks included the simultaneous 1986 gun-and-grenade attacks by the Libyan-backed Abu Nidal Organization (ANO) at airports in Rome and Vienna. Such attacks convinced authorities that security at all public transportation areas, including airports, railroad stations, and docks, needed to be improved. Public safety officials and law enforcement agencies began to coordinate intelligence about terrorist activities, together with information about how much aid and protection terrorists got from their sponsors.

Also in 1986, the International Civil Aviation Organization (ICAO), a non-governmental group of airline security experts, recommended that baggage belonging to

passengers who did not show up for a flight should be removed from the airplane in case it contained a bomb. The Lockerbie investigation revealed that such precautions were still not routine for most airlines by the end of 1988. The disaster forced many airlines to tighten up procedures involved in matching passengers and their bags.

The Use of Sanctions

For the most part, governments in the 1980s reacted to the revelation of links between states and terrorism with the only means available to them: diplomatic and economic sanctions against the offending country.

After the Lockerbie investigation made clear the key role of Gadhafi in the bombing, Libya was shunned by most Western governments. Trade links with Libya were severed, and diplomatic communications were restricted to contacts through third parties. The result of such moves, which were introduced by the UN under pressure from the United States and Great Britain, was to isolate Libya politically and economically. The country was forced to become almost self supporting as its international trade dried up. Even countries that remained friendly to Libya were afraid to demonstrate too close a relationship in case it resulted in them being punished for the association. Gadhafi, who liked to see himself as an international leader of Arab nationalism, found himself barely able to travel outside Libya.

In the past, however, sanctions—such as those imposed on Italy after its invasion of Ethiopia in 1936 or on the white-minority government of Rhodesia in the late 1960s—have often had only limited effect Some countries are usually willing to exploit an economic opportunity to trade illegally with states under sanctions. A further limitation of sanctions was apparent when they were imposed upon Iraq after its defeat in the Persian Gulf War in 1991. Although the sanctions were meant to undermine the regime of Saddam Hussein by weakening Iraq's economy, most of their effect fell on ordinary Iraqis, many of whom already lived in desperate poverty. Hussein and other officials continued to live in great luxury. The people who suffer most under non-specific sanctions are often those who have no say in the policies of their government.

Direct Action

Another option open to governments is direct military action. On April 14, 1986, for example, U.S. president Ronald Reagan ordered an air attack on Tripoli and Benghazi in Libya. The raids were in retaliation for Libya's part in the bombing of a disco in Berlin, Germany, which was used by U.S. service personnel. The aim of the raids was to kill Gadhafi himself.

Direct action, however, has its own risks. Under international law, it is illegal to try to assassinate state leaders or other officials, even if they openly sponsor terrorism. It is often difficult to gain support from other countries for such action. Military action might also serve only to inflame a situation by prompting responses, as happened after the Tripoli attack.

International Coalitions

The U.S. government found it easier to gain broad international support for

> **It is illegal to try to assassinate state leaders, even if they openly sponsor terrorism**

The Problem of Syria

Western governments have long known that Syria has sponsored terrorist groups opposed to the existence of Israel. Syria has also fought three wars—in 1948, 1967, and 1973—in attempts to destroy Israel. Israel occupied the Golan Heights, a strategically important area of high ground in southeastern Syria, during the 1967 war and has kept control of it since then.

Having failed to destroy Israel, Syria adopted a policy of supporting terrorist groups that sought to force an Israeli retreat from territory claimed by the Palestinians. Syria has funded and trained a number of terrorist groups, from the Palestine Liberation Organization (PLO) to the Palestinian Front for the Liberation of Palestine-General Command (PFLP-GC).

In recent years, the Syrian leadership has begun to curtail its support of terrorism, particularly after the death of President Hafiz al-Assad in 2000. Like Gadhafi in Libya, the new Syrian government indicated that it may consider a negotiated settlement that acknowledges Israel's right to exist.

Western governments welcomed Syria's apparent change of heart. One sign of approval was an official state visit to the country by British prime minister Tony Blair in October 2001.

▼ The image of President Hafiz al-Assad looms over a crowd at a soccer game in Syria in 1995. Assad openly sponsored terrorist groups for nearly thirty years.

The Taliban and Al-Qaeda

In the days after the September 11, 2001, attacks on United States, which destroyed the World Trade Center, damaged the Pentagon, and took thousands of lives, U.S. authorities quickly identified al-Qaeda as the group behind the atrocity. They also identified the Islamic fundamentalist Taliban regime in Afghanistan as the key sponsor of the group. The Taliban provided a refuge for al-Qaeda's leaders and also a center for its recruitment and training.

Al-Qaeda and the Taliban shared the belief that the culture and religion of Islam were under threat from worldwide forces. Both groups had developed their extreme brand of Islamic fundamentalism during their resistance to the Soviet occupation of Afghanistan during the 1980s.

When the Taliban took power in Afghanistan in 1996, it saw al-Qaeda as its natural ally, particularly because al-Qaeda's leader, Osama bin Laden, promised to use terrorist tactics against Western countries, which both groups saw as their enemies. The Taliban provided money, weapons, and training camps to enable al-Qaeda to carry out its terrorist campaign against Western targets.

▼ A Taliban commander (left) prepares to lead his forces to fight the U.S.-led invasion of Afghanistan in November 2001.

The U.S.-Saudi Relationship

Most of the September 11 terrorists were born in Saudi Arabia. The revelation was a blow to many Americans who had long seen Saudi Arabia as an ally of the United States. Saudi Arabia, for example, had served as a base for the international coalition that fought the successful U.S.-led 1991 campaign that forced Saddam Hussein's army out of Kuwait.

Many Americans wondered how a friendly nation could produce so many terrorists. Many Saudis, however, particularly followers of the strict Wahhabi form of Islam, see Western influence on their country as being against Islamic values. They reject, for example, what they see as Western consumerism and permissive social values. Some of them blame the United States and its allies for corrupting their Islamic society.

The U.S.-government commission that investigated the September 11 attacks concluded, in part, that some Saudis resented their country having a relationship with the United States based mainly on economic considerations. The commission recommended that the U.S. government should try to develop stronger social and cultural ties with the Saudi kingdom as a way of reducing ill-feeling toward the United States among ordinary Saudi citizens.

direct action after the terrorist attacks of September 11, 2001. This was partly because the attacks killed people from many countries and caused great outrage. It was also partly because it was easy to link the group that carried out the attack—the Islamist al-Qaeda organization—and the government that supported it in Afghanistan, where al-Qaeda had training camps and supply bases.

On September 12, George Robertson, secretary general of the North Atlantic Treaty Organization (NATO), invoked a collective security provision in NATO's constitution that said that an attack on any member of NATO was an attack on all of them and would be answered by all of them.

The clause had originally been intended to ensure united action against the spread of communism during the Cold War. The U.S. decision in 2001 to invade Afghanistan was also supported by many countries of the international community that were not members of NATO.

The invasion of Afghanistan demonstrated that Western governments were now prepared to make alliances even with states they regarded as having been sponsors of terrorism, as was the case with Pakistan. Pakistan's government had long been known to support terrorist groups in Kashmir, a disputed territory on its border with India. The country was also perceived by some as a

A Changed Dictator?

Ever since his apparent decision to end his policy of sponsoring terrorists, Colonel Mu'ammar Muhammad al-Gadhafi has been welcomed within the international community and Libya's political isolation has reduced.

Leaders of Western governments have gone to great lengths to prove to Gadhafi that acceptance in the international community offers great rewards. Governments around the world have lifted their diplomatic and economic sanctions against Libya; the country has been allowed to trade freely once again. In return, Gadhafi not only promised to end his sponsorship of terrorism, but also to give up Libya's program to develop weapons of mass destruction. Gadhafi also finally agreed to allow the two Libyan intelligence agents suspected of blowing up Pan Am 103 to stand trial, albeit in a special session of a Scottish court based in the Netherlands.

Despite Gadhafi's apparent repentance for past actions, other leaders did not entirely trust his change of heart. The U.S. government, in particular, was skeptical that Gadhafi would change. However, in June 2004, the United States acknowledged Gadhafi's progress by restoring diplomatic links with Libya after a period of twenty-four years.

supporter of al-Qaeda, which had many sympathizers among Pakistani Muslims.

Attracted by the potential economic and diplomatic advantages of joining the U.S.-led coalition, however, the leader of Pakistan's military regime, Pervez Musharraf, denounced violence and joined the war on terror. He provided coalition forces with a useful base next door to Afghanistan. After the war in Afghanistan, Pakistan continued to play a leading part in the campaign against al-Qaeda. It arrested a number of key al-Qaeda operatives who had taken shelter in Pakistan.

Some Western observers, however, doubt Pakistan's commitment to combating al-Qaeda in the long term. They point out that Musharraf is in a difficult position and has to carry out a careful balancing act. He is eager to cooperate with his U.S. allies, but he also needs to retain political support in Pakistan. Many Pakistani Muslims are hostile to the United States, which they see as having a harmful influence on the Islamic world.

Continuing Debate

There is still intense debate among analysts concerning the best approach to fighting state-sponsored terrorism. Should governments apply sanctions to force a policy change in the offending government? Or should they use direct

▲ Colonel Gadhafi (right) greets British prime minister Tony Blair in Tripoli in March 2004. The visit came after Gadhafi accepted responsibility for the Lockerbie bombing.

military action to bring down the offending regime? The renunciation of terrorism by Libya is an example of the apparent success of the former approach. The downfall of the Taliban regime in Afghanistan is an example of the second. Whatever the answer, it seems that, under a combination of economic and military pressure from the leading Western nations, fewer and fewer states around the world are opting to provide support to terrorists.

Libya's Rehabilitation

After Libya renounced terrorism and Gadhafi indicated that he wanted to rejoin the international community,

his gestures soon bore fruit. In March 2004, Tony Blair made an official visit to Libya, the first British prime minister to do so. The next month, Gadhafi visited the headquarters of the European Union in Brussels. Other regimes may well follow Gadhafi's example. Diplomatic and economic pressure from the international community continue to play a vital role in the decline of state-sponsored terrorism.

Time Line

1969 Colonel Muammar Muhammad al-Gadhafi takes power in Libya.

1986 April 14: The United States launches air strikes on targets in Libya.

1988 July 3: USS *Vincennes* shoots down an Iranian airliner, killing 290 people.
December 5: U.S. Embassy in Helsinki, Finland, receives a telephone warning of a bomb attack on a U.S. airliner.
December 21: A bomb destroys Pan Am Flight 103 over the Scottish village of Lockerbie, killing 270 people.

1990 October: Investigators identify two Libyans as the main suspects in the Lockerbie case.

1991 November 14: Indictments are issued against two chief suspects.

1992 United Nations imposes sanctions on Libya.

1999 April 5: Libya hands over the suspects for trial.

2001 January 31: Abdel Basset Al-Megrahi is sentenced to life imprisonment for the bombing; Lamin Khalifa Fhimah is acquitted.

2002 March: Al-Megrahi loses an appeal against the court's verdict.
August: Abu Nidal is found dead in Iraq.

2003 March: U.S.-led invasion of Iraq sparks ongoing insurgency, possibly backed by Syria.
August: Libya admits responsibility for Lockerbie bombing.
September: UN lifts sanctions on Libya.

2004 March: British prime minister Tony Blair visits Libya.
April: Gadhafi visits European Union headquarters in Brussels.

Glossary

compensation: payments made to make up for a wrongdoing.

counterterrorism: any actions intended to reduce terrorism or the threat of terrorism.

covert: secret, as in undercover military or police operations.

detonator: a device used for setting off an explosive.

extradition: the legal process of sending a person from one country to another in order to stand trial.

forensic: having to do with the use of scientific analysis in criminal investigations.

fuselage: the body of an airplane.

genocide: the organized killing of a whole race or other large group of people.

guerrilla war: a war fought by unconventional means, such as ambushes and small-scale attacks on scattered targets.

guillotine: a machine for execution that consists of a sharp blade that slides down inside a frame to behead the condemned person lying beneath.

insurgency: an unlawful uprising against civic authority.

Islamism: the belief that Islam should be the basis of all forms of government and culture

sanctions: international restrictions placed on a country's trade or diplomatic relations with other countries.

Semtex: a plastic explosive made in the form of a putty-like material.

surveillance: keeping close watch on someone or something.

timer: in a bomb, the part that controls when the detonator will spark an explosion.

warrant: a legal document required by security forces for certain actions, such as carrying out a search or making an arrest.

Further Reading

Books

Gunderson, Cory Gideon. *Terrorist Groups* (World in Conflict–The Middle East). Abdo and Daughters Publishing, 2003.

Harmon, Daniel E. *Libya* (Modern Middle East Nations and Their Strategic Place in the World). Mason Crest Publishers, 2003.

Miller, Debra A. *Libya* (Modern Nations of the World). Lucent Books, 2005.

Spies, Karen Bornemann. *Pan Am Flight 103: Terrorism over Lockerbie* (American Disasters). Enslow Publishers, 2003.

Wicker, Doug R. *The Bombing of Pan Am Flight 103* (Terrorist Attacks). Rosen Publishing Group, 2002.

Web Sites

BBC News Lockerbie Milestones
news.bbc.co.uk/1/hi/world/
1134471.stm

BBC News Lockerbie: Ten Years On
news.bbc.co.uk/1/hi/special_report/
1998/12/98/lockerbie/237035.stm

BBC News: Lockerbie Time Line
news.bbc.co.uk/1/hi/world/
740732.stm

CNN.com Special Report: The Lockerbie Bombing Trial
edition.cnn.com/LAW/trials.
and.cases/case.files/0010/lockerbie/

***Guardian* Unlimited Special Report: Lockerbie**
www.guardian.co.uk/Lockerbie/
0,2759,431005,00.html

***TIME* Trail: Lockerbie**
www.time.com/time/europe/
timetrails/lockerbie/index.html

Victims of Pan Am Flight 103
web.syr.edu/~vpaf103/

***Washington Post*.com Special Report: Pan Am 103**
www.washingtonpost.com/
wp-srv/inatl/longterm/panam103/
timeline.htm

Index